IT'S TIME TO EAT
APPLE DUMP CAKE

It's Time to Eat APPLE DUMP CAKE

Walter the Educator

Silent King Books
A WhichHead Entertainment Imprint

Copyright © 2024 by Walter the Educator

All rights reserved. No part of this book may be reproduced in any manner whatsoever without written per- mission except in the case of brief quotations embodied in critical articles and reviews.

First Printing, 2024

Disclaimer

This book is a literary work; the story is not about specific persons, locations, situations, and/or circumstances unless mentioned in a historical context. Any resemblance to real persons, locations, situations, and/or circumstances is coincidental. This book is for entertainment and informational purposes only. The author and publisher offer this information without warranties expressed or implied. No matter the grounds, neither the author nor the publisher will be accountable for any losses, injuries, or other damages caused by the reader's use of this book. The use of this book acknowledges an understanding and acceptance of this disclaimer.

It's Time to Eat APPLE DUMP CAKE is a collectible early learning book by Walter the Educator suitable for all ages belonging to Walter the Educator's Time to Eat Book Series. Collect more books at WaltertheEducator.com

USE THE EXTRA SPACE TO TAKE NOTES AND DOCUMENT YOUR MEMORIES

APPLE DUMP CAKE

It's time to eat, the table's set,

It's Time to Eat

Apple Dump Cake

A special treat we won't forget!

The smell is sweet, it's in the air,

Apple Dump Cake beyond compare!

Golden crust, all warm and bright,

Baked to perfection, just right tonight.

Soft apples hide beneath the top,

With cinnamon sprinkles that never stop.

Grab your fork and take a seat,

This is a dish that's fun to eat!

Scoop it out and watch it steam,

It's like a dessert from a dream.

The apples are soft, the topping's crisp,

A burst of flavor with every wisp.

The sugar and spice, they blend so well,

It's like a hug in every smell!

It's Time to Eat

Apple Dump Cake

Pile on some ice cream, make it grand,

Watch it melt, it's so unplanned!

The cold and warm, they mix so neat,

Together they make the perfect treat.

Let's share a plate and laugh a while,

Each bite brings a happy smile.

Friends and family all agree,

Apple Dump Cake is the key!

The clock strikes noon, or maybe night,

This tasty dish is always right.

For holidays or simple days,

It's sure to bring a round of praise.

So when you hear the oven beep,

You'll know it's time to take a leap.

Run to the table, don't be late,

It's Time to Eat

Apple
Dump
Cake

Apple Dump Cake will surely wait!

One last bite, let's savor slow,

The perfect end to the dessert show.

Thank you, apples, for being so sweet,

Time to eat was such a treat!

And don't forget, when it's all done,

Baking together is twice the fun!

We'll whip it up another day,

It's Time to Eat

Apple Dump Cake

Apple Dump Cake's here to stay!

ABOUT THE CREATOR

Walter the Educator is one of the pseudonyms for Walter Anderson. Formally educated in Chemistry, Business, and Education, he is an educator, an author, a diverse entrepreneur, and he is the son of a disabled war veteran. "Walter the Educator" shares his time between educating and creating. He holds interests and owns several creative projects that entertain, enlighten, enhance, and educate, hoping to inspire and motivate you. Follow, find new works, and stay up to date with Walter the Educator™

at WaltertheEducator.com

www.ingramcontent.com/pod-product-compliance
Lightning Source LLC
LaVergne TN
LVHW010622070526
838199LV00063BA/5239